Modern Industrial World

Russia

David Cumming

Thomson Learning

New York

MODERN INDUSTRIAL WORLD

France
Germany
Japan
Russia

Cover: Moscow lit up at night.
Title page: The Western-style GUM shopping mall in Moscow.
Contents page: Supporters of Boris Yeltsin demonstrate outside the Russian Parliament in Moscow during 1991.

First published in the
United States in 1995 by
Thomson Learning
115 Fifth Avenue
New York, NY 10003

First published in Great Britain in 1994 by
Wayland (Publishers) Ltd.

Library of Congress Cataloging-in-Publication Data
Cumming, David
  Russia / David Cumming.
     p.   cm. —(Modern industrial world)
  Includes bibliographical references and index.
  ISBN 1-56847-240-4
  1. Russia (Federation)—Economic conditions—1991-
—Juvenile literature. 2. Post-communism—Russia
(Federation)—Juvenile literature. [1. Russia (Federation)—
Economic conditions. 2. Post-communism—Russia
(Federation)] I. Title. II. Series.
HC340.12.C86   1994
330.947—dc20   94-26033

Printed in Italy

Contents

A vast country

Russia is the largest country in the world. Wrapped around the Northern Hemisphere, it occupies 17 percent of the earth, almost as much as the United States and Canada combined. Russia stretches 6,000 miles, from Europe in the west to the Pacific Ocean in the east. It is so wide that it spans eleven time zones. When people in Moscow are going to bed, those in Vladivostok on the Pacific coast are getting up the next day. The flight from Moscow to Vladivostok takes eight hours.

The low Ural Mountains, running north to south, split Russia into two unequal parts. Most of the people live in the smaller part on the western side of the Urals, where the best farm land and major industries are located. The larger part, east of the

Above *Shoppers in central Moscow, Russia's capital city.*

4

You can take the whole of the United States and set it down in the middle of Siberia… you can then take Alaska and all the countries of Europe, with the exception of Russia, and fit them into the remaining margin … you will still have more than 300,000 square miles of Siberian territory to spare. – George Kennan, an American journalist, writing in 1891

Below right

A Nenet girl feeds her reindeer in the frozen wastes of Siberia. The Nenets are a nomadic people.

Urals, is usually referred to as Siberia. Although Siberia is nearly one and a half times the size of the United States, its population is only one-tenth of the size. Siberia's harsh climate has kept settlers away and hindered development. Despite being rich in resources, the area remains a wilderness of thick forests, crisscrossed by innumerable rivers, and it is covered with snow and ice for much of the year.

LANDSCAPE AND CLIMATE

Because Russia is such a huge country, there are great variations in its landscape and climate. Most of it is flat, except for the mountainous regions of the Caucasus (on the eastern shores of the Black Sea) and eastern Siberia. On the Kamchatka Peninsula in eastern Siberia, there are many active volcanoes. This is also an area where earthquakes occur frequently.

Russia has four different types of landscape. Along its northern edge, mostly within the Arctic Circle, is the tundra, a windswept, treeless wasteland, bitterly cold in winter. Little can grow here apart from lichens and moss.

E R I A

S   I   A

Lena   ● Yakutsk

Baikal-Amur Mainline

Lake Baikal

Trans-Siberian Railway

● Kamchatka

MONGOLIA

● Vladivostok

I   N   A

PACIFIC OCEAN

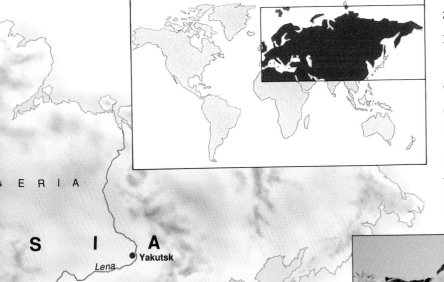

South of the tundra is the taiga, a wide belt of coniferous forests extending across the whole of central Russia. The most common trees are larch, pine, fir, and spruce. The pine needles and cones that fall from the trees make the soil acidic, so it is poor for farming. As in the tundra, much of the ground is permafrost – frozen to depths of nearly a mile. In the summer the top layer melts and forms mosquito-infested marshes.

Below the taiga is a narrow band of flat grasslands, known as steppe. The fertile black soil, called chernozem, is excellent for farming.

South of the steppe the land is semidesert. Little grows in this sandy soil unless it is irrigated by the nearby Volga River.

Much of Russia is nearer the North Pole than the equator, so it has a very cold climate, with snow on the ground and ice on the seas, rivers, and lakes for months on end. In northern Siberia the average temperature in January is -60°F, making it the coldest inhabited place in the world.

RUSSIA AT A GLANCE

Area: 6,592,819 square miles.

Capital: Moscow.

Population: 149,500,000 (females 53%, males 47%).

Population density: 23 people per square mile.

Main cities (population in millions): Moscow 8.8, St. Petersburg (formerly Leningrad) 4.5, Nizhny Novgorod (Gorky) 1.4, Novosibirsk 1.4, Yekaterinburg (Sverdlovsk) 1.3, Samara (Kuybyshev) 1.2, Omsk 1.1.

Religion: Mainly Christians; also Muslims, Jews, and Buddhists.

Language: Russian is the official language and the most widely spoken, although local people speak their own languages in their homelands.

Currency: Ruble, divided into 100 kopecks.

Highest point: Mount Elbrus (about 18,500 feet) in the Caucasus.

Longest rivers: Ob-Irtyush (9,080 miles), Lena (7,080 miles).

CIS: Russia is a member country of the Commonwealth of Independent States (CIS), along with Armenia, Azerbaijan, Belarus, Kazakhstan, Kyrgyzstan, Moldova, Tadjikistan, Turkmenistan, the Ukraine, and Uzbekistan – all former republics of the USSR.

The natural regions of Russia

ARCTIC OCEAN

• Yakutsk

URAL MOUNTAINS

Moscow

• Astrakhan

PACIFIC

OCEAN

KEY

Tundra

Taiga

Steppe

Mixed forest

Desert

Western Russia has shorter, less severe winters, with the temperature rarely dropping below 5°F. The far south, along the shores of the Black Sea and the Caspian Sea, is the warmest part of Russia. In summer temperatures can reach 95°F.

The wettest area is western Russia, which has up to 32 inches of rain annually. Southern and northern Siberia are the driest parts, with less than 16 inches of rain a year.

ONE COUNTRY, MANY PEOPLES

Today the correct name for Russia is the Russian Federation. It is divided into twenty-one republics, five regions, and ten areas, which roughly correspond to the traditional homelands of the largest groups of peoples living there. The Slavs are the largest group, making up 82 percent of the population. Their central European ancestors were the original settlers of western Russia; now they live all over the country. There are about one hundred other groups of people, of whom the 5.5 million Tatars are the largest. The Aleuts, fishing people on the Pacific coast, are the smallest group, numbering less than 500.

These Buryat people are farmers in their traditional homeland in southeast Siberia.

7

Past and present times

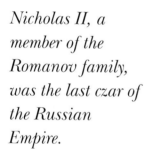

The vast empire of Russia was ruled from 1613 to 1917 by czars of the Romanov royal family. The Romanovs did little to improve living conditions for any but the richest people. Most of the population were peasant serfs without any rights, "tied" like slaves to landowners' estates. When an estate was sold, the serfs automatically became the property of the purchaser. Despite repeated calls for reform, serfdom was not abolished until 1861. Although free, the peasants continued to lead a miserable existence, uneducated and badly fed.

In 1914 Russia entered World War I, fighting alongside the United States, Great Britain, and France against Germany. It was soon obvious that Russia had not advanced as quickly as its allies. Let down by poor equipment and inadequate supplies, its armies faced defeat. Millions of extra troops had to be recruited in a hurry, mainly from the farming community. Consequently, food production dropped and Russians began to go hungry. By 1917 Russia was in crisis: its people were starving, and they

Nicholas II, a member of the Romanov family, was the last czar of the Russian Empire.

This painting shows the Tatars attacking Vladimir, near Moscow, in 1238. The Tatars ruled Russia until 1480, when they were conquered by Ivan the Great.

1240 Kiev destroyed by Tatars.

1480 Ivan the Great defeats the Tatars. Moscow the capital.

1547 Ivan the Terrible crowned the first czar.

1613 The first Romanov czar, Mikhail. Russia expands into an empire.

1712 Capital moved to St. Petersburg.

1917 Revolution overthrows Romanov family. Communist party takes over government, led by Lenin.

1918 Capital moved back to Moscow.

1922 Creation of the USSR.

1924 Lenin dies. Stalin replaces him as leader.

1941 Germany invades the USSR.

1943 German army defeated at Stalingrad (Volgograd).

1945 End of World War II.

1946 Cold war starts when the USSR refuses to leave eastern Europe.

1948 Berlin Blockade.

1953 Stalin dies.

1956 The USSR invades Hungary.

1968 Czechoslovakia invaded by the USSR.

1985 Gorbachev becomes the USSR's leader; introduces *perestroika* and *glasnost*.

1989 Yeltsin elected leader of the Russian Republic.

1991 Failed coup to overthrow Gorbachev. End of USSR; replaced by CIS (Commonwealth of Independent States). Gorbachev retires.

1993 Yeltsin closes the Russian Parliament. The first democratic elections since the end of communism.

1994 Opening of the new parliament.

Rebels patrol the streets of St. Petersburg during the 1917 Russian Revolution.

were furious with the czar and his generals for their incompetence on the battlefields, where thousands were dying daily. In March 1917 the Russian Revolution began. Workers went on strike in St. Petersburg, which was by then the capital of the Russian Empire. Soon workers in all the other cities followed their

Russian civilians fighting the army in Moscow in 1917. People had opposed czarist rule for many years before the 1917 revolution.

example. Troops were sent to restore order, but they mutinied and Czar Nicholas II had to abdicate.

A temporary government was formed by some members of the Duma (Parliament), but it was constantly criticized by Lenin, the leader of the Bolshevik political party. On November 7, the Bolsheviks stormed the Winter Palace in St. Petersburg and arrested the government.

LEADING PEOPLE IN RUSSIAN HISTORY

Lenin (Vladimir Ilyich Ulyanov) (1870 – 1924)

Lenin created the world's first communist country, putting into practice the ideas of Karl Marx. In 1848 Marx published *The Communist Manifesto*, which criticized capitalism as a way of running a country's economy. Marx said that a country should not be split into a class of rich people, who owned all the factories and land, and a class of poor people, who worked for them. Instead the nation (the state) should own all the land and industries, so that everyone would benefit equally from what was produced. Lenin adapted Marx's ideas to suit the USSR's needs, creating a type of communism known as Marxism-Leninism.

COMMUNIST RULE

In March 1918 the Bolshevik party renamed itself the Communist party. Its aim was to rid Russia of the injustices

Josef Stalin (1879–1953)

Stalin replaced Lenin as the leader of the Communist party and of the USSR in 1924. He became a cruel dictator, stopping at nothing to make the USSR one of the strongest military and industrial countries in the world. Anyone who opposed his plans was murdered or sent to a prison camp in Siberia. Millions died during his "reign of terror." He was responsible for collectivizing agriculture and speeding up the USSR's industrialization.

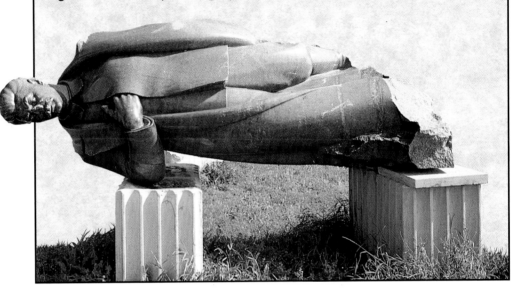

This statue of Stalin was pulled down soon after Russia's independence. Stalin is still hated forty years after his death. It is said that there is only one statue of him left in the whole of Russia and the CIS – in his hometown in Georgia.

of czarist times and to create a more equal society. The communist state took over ownership of all the land, industries, stores, houses, and the transportation system.

In 1922 the Russian Empire became the Union of Soviet Socialist Republics (USSR). Two years later Lenin died, and Josef Stalin replaced him as the leader of both the Communist party and the USSR. Stalin wanted the USSR to be an important industrial country, so he ordered the building of many large engineering and iron and steel factories, and the opening up of iron ore and coal mines. Consequently, when World War II broke out in 1939, the USSR was better equipped than during World War I. When the German army invaded the USSR in 1941, it advanced as far as Stalingrad. But in 1943, after a bloody and long-fought battle, it was forced to retreat, hotly pursued by the USSR's Red Army, which helped the United States and its

11

The division of Europe after World War II

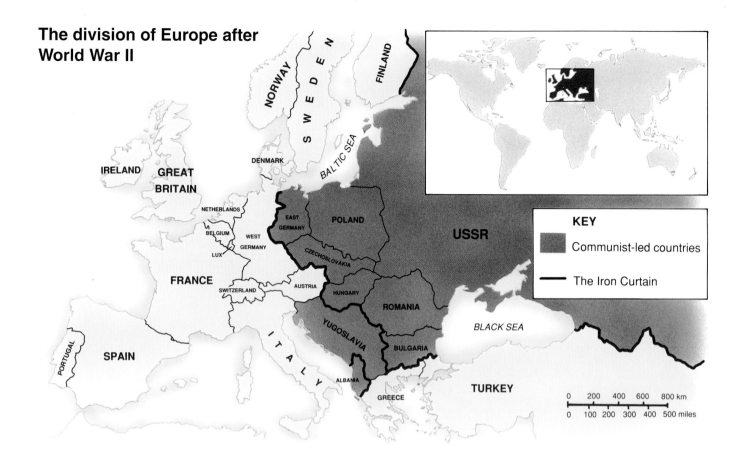

After World War II, Europe was split into the communist east and the noncommunist west. The Iron Curtain that separated them was finally dismantled during the late 1980s when the peoples of East European countries rebelled against the Communist party.

allies to capture Berlin in 1945. By then the Red Army had invaded all the countries Germany had occupied: Romania, Hungary, Bulgaria, Poland, Czechoslovakia, and Yugoslavia. It also controlled the eastern half of Germany.

Although the USSR had fought with the United States to defeat Germany, Stalin was determined to spread communism into Europe, so he refused to move out of the territories gained by the Red Army.

After the end of World War II, a dividing line, the Iron Curtain, was drawn across Europe through Germany, which was divided into two. To the west of the Iron Curtain were noncommunist countries. To its east were USSR-controlled countries, which were forced to become communist.

If, after forty years of communism, a person cannot have a glass of milk or a pair of shoes, he will not believe that communism is a good thing, no matter what you tell him.
– Nikita Khrushchev, the USSR's leader from 1957 to

Together these communist countries became known as the Eastern Bloc.

Once allies against a common enemy, the United States and the USSR became rivals, each convinced that its system of government and industrial organization was the better. Both began to spend enormous sums of money on weapons in an arms race to become the most powerful country in the world.

THE BREAKUP OF THE USSR

The rivalry and mistrust that developed between the USSR and the U.S. in postwar years is known as the cold war. The cold war continued until 1985, when Mikhail Gorbachev became the USSR's leader. By then the USSR was advancing at a much slower pace than the other major industrial countries. So much money was being spent on arms, there was little left to modernize its factories or to build new ones to provide people with the everyday things that were taken for granted in noncommunist countries.

Gorbachev called a halt to the cold war and began negotiations with the United States to end the arms race. As less money was spent on arms, more became available to invest in industry.

Far right
Mikhail Gorbachev, former leader of the USSR. His reforms won him popularity abroad but not in his own country.

LEADING PEOPLE IN RUSSIAN HISTORY

Mikhail Gorbachev (1931–   )
President of the USSR from 1985 to 1990, Gorbachev was responsible for ending the cold war between the USSR and the United States, for which he won a Nobel Peace Prize. His attempts at reforming the USSR through *perestroika* and *glasnost* made him unpopular. The end of communism and the breakup of the USSR left him with no job, so he retired, although there are rumors that he might reenter politics.

Boris Yeltsin (1931–   )
In 1989 Yeltsin was elected president of the Russian Republic. In 1991 he opposed a coup against Gorbachev and then became the leader of the newly independent Russia. He plans to make Russia a democratic capitalist country. Until now, ex-members of the Communist party in Parliament have opposed his reforms. In September 1993 Yeltsin closed Parliament and ordered elections in the hope of making the ex-communists less powerful. They managed to maintain their power, however.

Russians demonstrate their support for Boris Yeltsin outside Parliament during the Communist party's attempted coup against Mikhail Gorbachev in 1991. Boris Yeltsin persuaded the army not to support the coup and it failed.

In the late 1980s the Eastern Bloc countries began demanding an end to one-party government by the Communist party. In the past such behavior had been dealt with severely. For example, in 1956 the Red Army had been sent into Hungary to put down a rebellion. Gorbachev, however, allowed free elections to be held, and one by one the Eastern Bloc countries voted for noncommunist governments that would no longer be controlled by the USSR.

Encouraged by this, the republics within the USSR demanded independence and an end to communism. The Communist party was not pleased, and in the summer of 1991 it led a coup against Mikhail Gorbachev in an attempt to restore the Party's control of the USSR. The coup failed because Boris Yeltsin, president of the Russian republic, persuaded the army not to support the rebels.

By the end of 1991 the republics had declared independence and the USSR had ceased to exist. Eleven of its former republics set up the Commonwealth of Independent States (CIS), under Russia's leadership, with the intention of maintaining close links in the future. The new countries of Georgia, Lithuania, Estonia, and Latvia decided not to join.

Trade and industry

A steel mill in the Ukraine produces red-hot metal. Heavy industries, like iron and steel making, were a priority in the USSR's command economy.

A COMMAND ECONOMY

In 1918 the USSR had very few industries. Compared to Europe and the United States, it was an undeveloped nation: more people worked on farms than in factories. Within fifty years, the Communist party had created one of the most powerful economies in the world. It was able to do this so quickly because under communism the state owned all the natural resources, mines, and

RUSSIA'S GNP
GNP (1993): $24.1 billion
GNP per capita (1993): $2,100

industries. This meant that the government could decide which industries to develop, where they would be built, and how much they would produce. Its decisions were published in five-year plans, which set targets for industries to meet.

The system under which the USSR's industries were run is called a command

15

Automobile industry in Togliatti

In the 1960s the Italian firm Fiat helped the Russians build a new car factory at Togliatti. When completed, it was the largest factory in Russia and one of the largest in the world. Most of the cars sold in Russia are made here, as are the majority of Russian cars sold abroad.

The factory was built at Togliatti for the following reasons:
• Togliatti is situated midway between the two largest iron and steel making regions – the Donbas (to the north of the Black Sea, now in the Ukraine) and the cities along the eastern edge of the Ural Mountains, of which Magnitogorsk is the most important. Together these regions supply the factory with all the metals it needs to build automobiles. The iron and steel are transported by train to Togliatti; the Ural metals are sent on the Trans-Siberian Railway.
• Manufacturing automobiles requires huge amounts of electricity and water. Both of these are supplied by the nearby Volga River. The Lenin Dam is close to Togliatti, and hydroelectric power generated there is taken by grid to the factory. The dam has created a large reservoir, from which water can be piped to the factory throughout the year.

Togliatti is ideally situated for an automobile factory. Once built, the cars do not have to be transported far to their owners, since most people live in western Russia.

In the past important government and Communist party officials traveled in limousines like this one. Now, only the rich can afford to own cars.

• Togliatti is near Kuybyshev, the sixth-largest city in Russia, with a population of 1.2 million. This meant that finding workers for the new factory was no problem.

• Togliatti is in western Russia, where most of the population live. Once built, automobiles do not have to be transported great distances to their owners, which would have been the case if the factory had been built in Siberia.

• Togliatti is also closer to Europe than Siberia is. One of the reasons for building the factory was to increase the sales of Russian cars in Europe, as well as in Russia.

Before the Togliatti factory was built, cars were very expensive in Russia and people had to wait several years for delivery. The Togliatti factory has lowered the price of cars and shortened the waiting time. Yet the demand for new cars remains higher than output. In the future, U.S. and European car manufacturers such as Ford and Volkswagen will probably open factories in Russia to enable millions more people to become car owners.

economy. This is the opposite of the market economy found in capitalist countries like the United States and Great Britain. In capitalist countries the state owns only a few industries, the majority being in the hands of private companies. The government controls its own industries but lets private firms do what they want. Private companies in a market economy compete with one another to produce goods and services people (consumers) want to buy. People make their choices based on the quality and the price of what is offered.

Eager consumers line up to get into a Western clothes store in Moscow. Private businesses like this one are a feature of a market economy.

Because they operate in different ways, command and market economies do not develop along the same lines. In a market economy the consumers influence what will be produced. In a command economy it is the government that decides. In the USSR the government and the Communist party were one and the same in all but name, since all government officials had to be Party members. So the government did what the Party wanted. The Party made the government invest most of its money in two areas. The first was heavy industries, such as the manufacture of iron and steel, factory machinery, and the extraction of natural resources, like coal, oil, and minerals. The second area was arms and space research. The Party considered the production of consumer goods like televisions and washing machines much less important.

It was not until the late 1960s that the Communist party began to attach any importance to consumer goods. Between then and the mid-1980s their manufacture doubled. But factories could not produce enough to satisfy people's needs. When Mikhail

DISTRIBUTION OF LABOR	
Industry & construction	42.8%
Science, education, arts, health, social security	19.5%
Agriculture & forestry	13.4%
Transportation & communication	7.9%
Government & finance	2.3%
Others	14.1%

Gorbachev became the leader of the USSR in 1985, only about 10 percent of all the money invested in industries was spent on consumer goods factories. At that time in the United States – whose population was not even twice that of the USSR – there were twelve times as many cars and nine times as many telephones. The United States had been able to expand its production of consumer goods at the same time as expanding heavy industries, arms production, and space research.

TRADING PARTNERS

On his frequent trips abroad, Gorbachev became increasingly aware that the USSR's economy was lagging far behind that of noncommunist countries. More importantly, these countries were reluctant to trade with the USSR because the goods it produced were old-fashioned and poorly made.

In recent years Russia has improved the design and quality of tractors to win more customers abroad.

The USSR's main trading partners were other Communist countries, particularly the ones in the Eastern Bloc. In 1949 they had set up the Council for Mutual Economic Assistance (COMECON), which coordinated the development of all their industries so that there was no overlap in production. Instead of every member country making railroad cars, for example, East Germany concentrated on this area of manufacture. From there they were exported to other COMECON countries, which did not pay for the cars but instead exchanged goods of equivalent value. This system, involving no money, is called bartering. Since there was no competition between them, the COMECON countries had no incentive to produce well-made goods that were superior to those made by another country. While poor-quality goods were tolerated within the Eastern Bloc and the

RUSSIAN TRADE		
	% of imports	% of exports
Machinery & light industrial equipment.....	56.5	43
Food & grains	21	4
Chemicals..	7.5	11
Iron, steel, & other metals..........................	7	12
Petroleum & gas.......................................	2	15
Wood & paper	1.5	6
Others	4.5	9

A woman begs outside a new pizza restaurant in Moscow. Perestroika *encouraged foreign firms to invest in Russia, but many of them charge prices the poor cannot afford.*

USSR, they stood little chance of being sold in world markets, where other countries and multinational firms rivaled one another to produce the best.

PERESTROIKA

The advance of the USSR's industries was held back not only by COMECON but also by the command structure within the economy. The five-year plans for production were drawn up in Moscow, far away from the factories, by officials who were often out of touch with what was needed. Warehouses began to fill up with machinery factories could not use and goods people did not want to buy.

Mikhail Gorbachev decided it was time to restructure the command economy. He called this *perestroika.* Factory managers were given more freedom to make decisions – in effect, to make their own five-year plans – as long as they met the overall targets set by Moscow. Factories within each industry were encouraged to compete to produce high-quality goods. Some of the profit earned from selling them could be kept by the factory instead of being given to the government as before. This money could be used to

This shipyard on the Volga River has recently been privatized. The collapse of the Russian economy means it must now try to get work from outside Russia.

buy new equipment or to pay employees bonuses for working hard.

Gorbachev also opened the USSR to foreign firms. Many U.S., European, and Japanese companies set up partnerships with USSR businesses in return for being allowed to trade there. Gorbachev hoped that this exchange of ideas and technology would help the USSR to increase its production of consumer goods, as well as improve its ability to trade all over the world.

AFTER COMMUNISM

Though much of the command economy remains in place, many factories have now been sold to workers' cooperatives or private companies. They can operate without government interference. Over the next few years the government plans to sell off more of its industries. Exactly how many has yet to be decided, although it is thought that Russia will eventually be like most other capitalist countries,

Gold that was mined in Yakutia, Siberia, where most of Russia's gold resources lie.

with few government-owned industries and many private ones.

The move from communism to capitalism has brought many problems. Many factories that worked well under communism are struggling to compete with more advanced foreign firms and their future hangs in the balance. Government subsidies once propped up inefficient firms, but most of these have been stopped or reduced severely, leaving firms on the edge of bankruptcy, unable to pay their workers, and with little money to continue manufacturing. Throughout Russian industry, production has slumped alarmingly. It has been estimated that the introduction of capitalism may cause up to 20 million workers to lose their jobs.

With the breakup of the Eastern Bloc in 1991, COMECON came to an end. COMECON had shielded Russia from the outside world: whatever it produced could be bartered for something else. Now the old Eastern Bloc countries are looking for new trading partners, and Russia must compete with them. Although the members of the CIS have strong trade links with Russia, they are also turning to other countries for trade.

As well as updating its industries, Russia has to create all the institutions and services that support capitalism. A stock market has been opened in Moscow, with branches in other large cities. New banks that specialize in providing business loans have been created. A national telecommunications network is being installed to allow firms and factories to communicate by fax and to transfer information among computers. Business schools have been opened to train managers in the ways of capitalism.

It is early but, given time and a lot of money, Russia has the potential to become one of the most advanced industrial countries in the world.

RESOURCE RICH

The reason Russia will become an important country in the next century is that it is very rich in natural resources. It has more than 30 percent of the world's known gas reserves and it is the world's main producer of iron ore. There are also huge deposits of coal, oil, manganese, nickel, tin, gold, diamonds, and other precious minerals. The main problem is that most of these resources are in Siberia, while the industries in need of them are far away in western Russia, across the other side of the Ural Mountains.

Railroads are the best means of transporting most of Siberia's resources to the west, since the rivers and Arctic Ocean are frozen for up to nine months of the year. It is difficult to build roads because the ground is marshy in summer when the permafrost melts. Besides, the huge distances involved make road transportation too expensive to be worthwhile. The Trans-Siberian Railway, opened in 1914, connects Moscow with Vladivostok, a distance of 5,600 miles – the longest railroad line in the world. Late in the 1980s the Trans-Siberian was joined by the Baikal-Amur Mainline. However, most of Siberia remains out of reach of railroads. Whether any more can be built, bearing in mind the cost and difficult terrain, is questionable, at least within the near future.

Russia has large deposits of several important resources, which it can use for its own industries or for export.

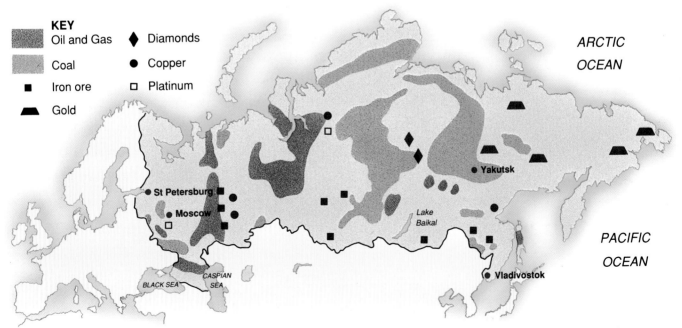

KEY
- Oil and Gas
- Coal
- ■ Iron ore
- ◣ Gold
- ◆ Diamonds
- ● Copper
- ☐ Platinum

ARCTIC OCEAN

PACIFIC OCEAN

St Petersburg
Moscow
Yakutsk
Lake Baikal
Vladivostok
BLACK SEA
CASPIAN SEA

Using the land

Russia's main crops and where they are located.

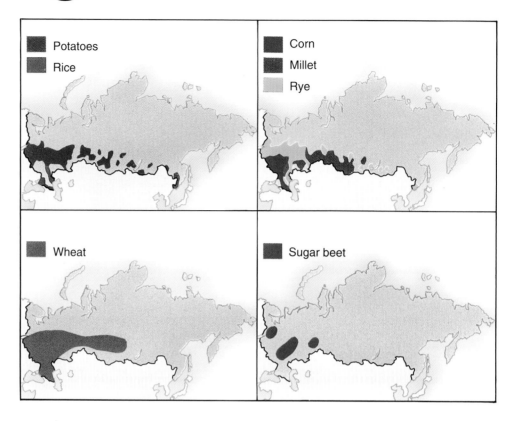

| Potatoes |
| Rice |

| Corn |
| Millet |
| Rye |

| Wheat |

| Sugar beet |

LAND USE

Forests	45%
Farmland	25%
Unfarmable land	30%

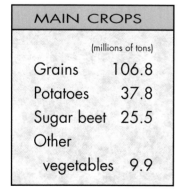

MAIN CROPS

(millions of tons)

Grains	106.8
Potatoes	37.8
Sugar beet	25.5
Other vegetables	9.9

The freezing climate of the tundra and the poor soil of the taiga mean that only a small area to the west of the Ural Mountains can be used for farming. Before the 1917 revolution, food was produced on small peasant farms. Food shortages were common. In the late 1920s the Communist party took over ownership of all the land and agricultural equipment. The small farms were combined into large collective farms, called kolkhozy. Each kolkhoz comprised about a hundred peasant farms.

Kolkhozy had a mixture of crops and animals. Everything they produced was bought by the state. The more they produced, the greater their income. Any profits were shared equally among the workers.

The Communist party also created state farms, or sovkhozy. They were much larger than kolkhozy and specialized in one crop or in one breed of animal.

On both types of farms the state provided all the machinery, fertilizers, and seeds. The state also gave kolkhoz

24

LIVESTOCK	
	(millions)
Poultry	659.8
Sheep & goats	58.2
Cattle	57.0
Pigs	38.3
Horses	2.6

This farmer works on a sovkhoz specializing in sheep breeding on the northern coast of the Black Sea.

and sovkhoz workers a plot of land to cultivate for themselves. If they grew more than they needed, they could sell the extra fruit and vegetables at markets and keep the money.

The government realized in the 1980s that farmers were more productive if they were working for themselves rather than for the state. So it encouraged farmers to form private cooperatives that lease kolkhozy or sovkhozy from the state. In 1992 there were about 184,000 private farms in Russia.

THE DISAPPEARING TAIGA

Twice as large as the rain forests of the Amazon, Russia's taiga contains over 50 percent of the world's coniferous forests and 25 percent of its trees. The taiga covers over 2.3 million square miles, about 80 percent of which are in Siberia. Between 1966 and 1988, 20 percent of Siberia's taiga was destroyed.

Siberian forests do not contain the teeming, noisy masses of life found in tropical rainforests …But their destruction could create huge areas of bog as permafrost melts, and have just as serious an effect on world climate as the loss of tropical forests.
– Fred Pearce, Independent (London), *March 28, 1993*

Food shortages

These vegetables are from a kolkhoz in the delta of the Volga River on the northern shores of the Caspian Sea. Tomatoes, eggplant, peppers, and melons are grown in the fertile sandy soil that is irrigated by water from the Volga. Yet, there is a shortage of fresh fruit and vegetables in Russia. In 1988 it was estimated that 30 percent of Russia's farm produce was thrown away. It was never sold because it rotted on the way to markets and stores. Despite changes in agriculture, many fruit and vegetables still never reach people.

In the USSR agriculture was part of the command system. Targets for crop production were issued as part of an overall five-year plan established in Moscow. Orders were then passed down the line to the kolkhozy. The weakness of the system was that it was unable to coordinate both the production of crops and their distribution. A kolkhoz might have its harvest ready for collection, but there would be no trucks or trains to transport it. The kolkhoz had done its job. Distributing its crops was someone else's responsibility. The kolkhoz was paid by the government for meeting its targets, irrespective of how much of its harvest was sold.

The poor distribution system meant that if harvests failed in one region, the government found it difficult to transfer crops to it from a region where the harvest had been better. Thus, some cities had plenty of food, while those in a neighboring region went without.

Today many kolkhozy are being forced to stand on their own, without any government help. The kolkhozy are responsible not only for growing crops but also for distributing and selling them. The money they earn

PRIVATE VS. STATE LAND PRODUCTION

	% of farm land	% of food production
Private plots	3%	25%
State & collective farms	97%	75%

comes from selling their harvests. What is important now is not how much they produce but how much they sell.

In the USSR more money was invested in industry than in farming. As a result, kolkhozy do not have enough trucks to take their crops to markets. Using trucks is very expensive because of the high price of diesel and gasoline. In the USSR, much of the harvesting was done by students and schoolchildren, who were paid no money. Now, if

These vegetables were grown on a kolkhoz on the northern shores of the Caspian Sea. The kolkhoz has a good harvest, but much of its produce never reaches the markets because of Russia's poor distribution system.

kolkhozy need help at harvest time, people have to be paid. Without money for new trucks, fuel, or extra workers, kolkhoz farmers like the ones in the delta have to leave crops to rot.

As well as removing the natural habitats of animals and birds, the destruction of the taiga is disrupting the traditional life-styles of the native people of Siberia. Many of them are reindeer herders, who are now finding massive logging camps in the middle of the land where they have grazed their animals for centuries. In the 1970s one state logging company was even allowed to build a new town, complete with its own airport and hydroelectric plant, supplied by a dam that flooded hundreds of square miles of taiga.

The loss of the taiga's trees has extremely far-reaching consequences. Recent research shows that 10 percent of the world's carbon dioxide, produced by burning fossil fuels, is absorbed by the taiga. The more the forests shrink, the less carbon dioxide the taiga will remove from the atmosphere and the greater will be the impact of global warming. In addition, when trees are removed the permafrost beneath them melts more quickly, turning the land into marsh. This emits methane, another dangerous greenhouse gas.

Each year about 10 million acres of Siberia's taiga are cut down to make paper and building materials. The hillside on the right of the road has been stripped of trees.

A group of Nentsy herders discuss a gas company's plans to develop a gas field on their territory in Siberia.

At the present rate of loss, there will be little of the taiga left in Siberia by 2050. Russia is torn between listening to conservationists' arguments and earning much-needed money. So far there has been little planting of new trees to replace felled ones. Even if this were increased, it would take decades to make up for past mistakes because trees grow very slowly in Siberia's cold climate.

POLLUTION

Some of the taiga's timber is taken to Lake Baikal, in southern Siberia, where the Communist party built two large paper mills. Lake Baikal is the world's oldest and deepest lake. Many of the 2,000 species of animals and plants living in and around it are unique. Once its waters were so pure that they were crystal clear to a depth of 130 feet. Today, because of the poisonous waste from the paper mills, the water is murky and the fish and plants are dying.

The pollution of Lake Baikal is typical of the Communist party's lack of concern for the environment in its haste to industrialize the USSR. Although laws have been passed to reduce pollution, Russia does not have the money to modernize its industries. Current estimates reveal that 25 percent of drinking water is harmful and that 20 percent of the population live in areas with dangerously high levels of air pollution.

St. Petersburg women are giving birth to fewer and less healthy babies than a decade ago. ... What we are eating and breathing has made some couples unable to reproduce – women are not able to conceive, and younger men are impotent.
– Yelena Khmelevskaya, maternity specialist, St. Petersburg Press, *August 10, 1993*

An uncertain future

The Communist party rocketed the USSR into the twentieth century. In a relatively short period of time it transformed a predominantly peasant society dependent on agriculture into one of the world's major industrial powers. Yet, in doing so, the Party sowed the seeds for its own destruction.

Communism required great sacrifices from the people, not the least of which was an almost total control of their daily lives from the cradle to the grave. In return they were given a basic, but very low, standard of living. Housing, clothing, food, and travel costs were minimal; education and welfare facilities were free; jobs were for life. Increasingly, the people felt they had been given a raw deal. They had tightened their belts to help the USSR industrialize; now they wanted a life-style similar to that in capitalist democracies. Communism could not provide them with this.

Homeless people camp in Red Square, Moscow. Russia has a serious shortage of housing.

A MIXED ECONOMY?

Russia wants to replace communism with a capitalist economy, but seventy years of communism cannot be wiped out overnight. Presently Russia is in confusion, midway between communism and capitalism, with a leadership unsure of how fast to proceed and people debating where Russia is heading. Some are now wondering whether capitalism should be Russia's goal, suggesting instead a mixture of communism and capitalism. Within this mixed economy,

there would be many private firms, but most of the large and important industries would be owned by the state. While the politicians argue, daily life becomes tougher for the people.

*Can Russia rescue itself by finding some "third way" between socialism and capitalism? Not according to Marek Dabrowski, a Polish economist: "There is no third way." Nor does he believe that a "way back" to the old days of the command economy is feasible. "I don't see any way back. Some political forces may try, but they won't be successful." – **Peter Torday**,* **Independent (London)**, *March 14, 1993*

Communist party supporters protest against rising prices. They want a return to old times, when the Party kept the cost of living low.

WILL RUSSIA ITSELF SPLIT UP?

Russia contains many different peoples who were kept together in one country by the Communist party. Although it granted them some freedom in deciding matters for themselves, the Party made sure that they did not become too powerful. With the Party gone, many people want to break away from Russia and make their regions and republics independent countries. For example, the Muslim Tatars want a new independent Islamic country, Tatarstan, which would be in the middle of Russia. At the moment the Russian government is trying to prevent disintegration by giving peoples like the Tatars greater decision-making powers.

RUSSIA AND THE CIS

Russia's internal problems are not helped by the situation in neighboring CIS countries. As in Russia, the transition to capitalism and democracy is causing enormous upheavals. Like Russia, they too are all bankrupt. The Communist party

31

Yakutia — a new country?

Yakutia is the largest republic in Russia. The size of India, it takes up much of eastern Siberia. It is the traditional homeland of the Yakut people, who were conquered in the seventeenth century by Russian armies advancing to the shores of the Pacific Ocean. Yakutia has a population of one million, 50 percent of whom are Russians and 33 percent Yakuts. Although fewer in number, the Yakuts could play a vital role in Russia's future.

For hundreds of years, the Yakuts have been ruled by the Russians, who have done little to develop their republic, despite its being rich in resources. In addition to diamonds and gold, it has large deposits of oil and gas. Almost all of Russia's gold and 25 percent of the world's diamonds are mined in Yakutia. Until recently, the Yakuts had little control over what was done with their land's wealth. For example,

This woman and her daughter live in Yakutia, an area rich in gold, diamonds, and oil. Money from the sale of these resources goes directly to Moscow. Many Yakuts want their homeland to break away from Russia so that they can have more control over their land's wealth.

made all the USSR's republics interdependent to prevent them from breaking away. Iron ore mined in one republic was turned into iron and steel in another, which was used to make vehicles and machines in a third republic. Even though the republics have separated, they still have to rely

32

nearly all the money earned from the sale abroad of gold and diamonds remained in Moscow, with little being returned to Yakutia. Understandably, this has annoyed the Yakuts. They believe the resources in their lands belong to them. Therefore, the Yakuts argue, they should keep all the money from their sale. The Russian government disagrees. Although it now gives Yakutia a larger share of its resources' earnings, the Yakuts are not satisfied.

Many Yakuts now think that the only solution is for Yakutia to become an independent country. Then Yakutia would have total control over the sale of its resources and it would keep all the earnings for itself. Russia does not want this to happen. An independent Yakutia could choose with whom it wanted to do business and what prices it would charge. For example, if the United States were prepared to pay more than Russia for diamonds or oil, Russia would lose out. Also, Russia fears that if Yakutia breaks away, other Siberian regions will follow.

With most of the resources in western Russia nearly at an end, Russia depends on Siberia's resources for its future development. Early in 1994 Russian and U.S. engineers began discussing building a railroad tunnel between Siberia and Alaska. If the tunnel is constructed, it would be very easy for Yakutia to trade with North America, perhaps even easier than dealing with western Russia. Yakutia might then decide to become independent.

Fish is hung up to dry as preparation for the long winter in northern Yakutia.

on one another for the survival of their industries. The main difference is that now they have to pay for the materials transferred among them. Each former USSR republic is running up debts with the others while they try to sort themselves out.

Member States of the Commonwealth of Independent States (CIS)

AR	=	AUTONOMOUS REPUBLIC
AG	=	AUTONOMOUS REGION
AA	=	AUTONOMOUS AREA

Russia
1 Bashkir AR
2 Buryat AR
3 Dagestan AR
4 Yakut AR
5 Kabardino-Balkar AR
6 Kalmyk AR
7 Karelia AR
8 Komi AR
9 Mari AR
10 Mordvinia AR
11 North Ossetia AR
12 Tatar AR
13 Checheno-Ingush AR
14 Chuvash AR
15 Tuva AR
16 Udmurt AR
17 Adygei AG
18 Khakass AG
19 Gorno-Altai AG
20 Jewish AG (Birobidzhan)
21 Karachai-Circassia AG
22 Aginsky-Buryat AA
23 Khanty-Mansi AA
24 Dolgano-Nenetz AA
25 Evenki AA
26 Yamalo-Nenetz AA
27 Komi-Permyak AA
28 Koryak AA
29 Nenetz AA
30 Chukot AA
31 Ust-Ordinsky-Buryat AA

Azerbaijan
32 Nakhichevan AR
33 Nagorno-Karabakh AG

Tajikistan
34 Gorno Badakhshan AG
Uzbekistan
35 Kara-Kalpak AR

Georgia (had not joined the CIS by July 1992 but has indicated interest in doing so)

36 Abkhazia AR
37 Adzhar AR
38 South Ossetia AG

CIS member countries. Before 1991 all these areas were within the USSR.

FOREIGN AID

It has been estimated that it would cost $200 billion to stabilize Russia's economy. The industrialized countries of the world have promised Russia $24 billion to date. Further aid will be given only if they are satisfied that the government is capable of leading Russia through the difficult times ahead. Judging by the disorder surrounding the December 1993 elections, this has yet to be proved. Without a strong and stable government within an effective democracy, Russia is lost. Given firm leadership, foreign aid and investment can be channeled into making Russia one of the most advanced countries in the next century.

Life today

Russia is in the middle of yet another revolution. Excited by the prospects of a better and easier existence, the Russian people wholeheartedly rejected communism and the tight grip it had on their lives. Already many of them are regretting their decision. Neither wholly communist nor completely capitalist and democratic, Russia is in chaos. Life was hard under communism, but, for the majority of people, it is even tougher now.

HIGH PRICES, LOW INCOMES

Under communism, the state subsidized the cost of living so that everything was very cheap. Although wages were not high, people could buy basic necessities without difficulty. In 1992 the government withdrew all its subsidies, apart from

This woman scavenges bread from a garbage dump because she cannot afford to buy food. Incomes have not kept up with rising prices, and millions of Russians are struggling to survive.

The very wealthy, mostly shady biznesmeni *and racketeers, drive around Moscow in brand-new Mercedes and BMW limousines, and go to glittering dinner dances where unemployed musicians are grateful for a few roubles. The very poor beg on the streets or go out to the city rubbish tip to sift through stinking refuse for edible leftovers or saleable junk. The old ladies who hold out their hands for alms have to give a cut to the mafia. Those who scavenge at the dump have to hand over their best finds to the "boss" who sits in a rotting armchair at the base of the heap.*
– Helen Womack, **Independent (London),** *November 29, 1992*

those on some foods, and it let stores and businesses charge their own prices. Consequently, prices shot up. In 1993 they rose, on average, by 2,000 percent; a doubling or trebling of prices overnight was common. Incomes have not kept up with these increases. Russian society is now divided into a minority of rich people and a majority of poor people, and the gap between them grows larger every day.

Two heroin addicts in an apartment in Leningrad. The Russian mafia has encouraged the spread of drug abuse, both within Russia and in neighboring countries.

CORRUPTION AND CRIME INCREASE

The division between rich and poor is nothing new. Many people have referred to communism as the "big lie" because it did not create a society in which everyone was equal, even though that was its main aim. Under communism, members of the USSR's Communist party (about 10 percent of the population) had a comfortable life-style. They had access to goods and services unavailable to nonmembers. For example, they could travel abroad and they could buy Western clothes and food in special stores. Job promotion was easier for Party members, as was skipping the long lines for cars and homes.

Of course, non-Party members were well aware of the inequalities, but criticizing the Communist party was not tolerated. The people were kept under control by a strong police force with a wide network of informers. In Stalin's day criticism of the Communist party resulted more often than not in death; in more recent times it led to a prison-camp sentence in the frozen wastes of Siberia.

In the new Russia the police have become decentralized. Coupled with growing poverty, this has resulted in a soaring crime wave and the introduction of a new element into Russian society: the mafia. There has always been corruption in Russia. A shortage of many essential goods, combined with restrictions on the sale of foreign ones, created a thriving black market where officially unobtainable goods could be purchased illegally – if you had the money. Party members could often be "persuaded" to do something for you if you gave them money.

Young people compete to sell their goods in an open-air market. Under communism, this would have been discouraged.

The increase in the cost of living, unmatched by increases in income, has forced people at all levels of society to supplement their wages with bribes. When government officials block plans for new factories, payment of a bribe removes all obstacles. Space is found on "fully booked" trains by paying the ticket clerk extra money. Gangsters have recently taken charge of whole city neighborhoods. The police are paid to turn a blind eye to their activities. Moscow is now considered to be one of the most dangerous cities in the world. In 1993 an international organization canceled a conference there, fearing for the safety of its delegates.

IMPROVEMENTS IN DAILY LIFE
Although the end of communism has caused hardship, it has brought many changes that are improving daily life.

In the USSR there was strict censorship. Anything taught in schools or appearing in print or on television had to

Illegal sturgeon fishermen escape with their haul on the Volga River.

Black gold

The fish in the bottom of this boat are illegally caught sturgeon. Every year, between April and June, tens of thousands of sturgeon swim up the Volga to lay their black eggs, called caviar. Ninety percent of the world's caviar-producing sturgeon lay their eggs in the Caspian Sea.

Caviar is a luxury food. In Russia, caviar is known as black gold because it is as rare and precious as that metal. A medium-sized fish (like the ones in the photograph) is worth hundreds of dollars; a large one, thousands of dollars.

All sturgeon belong to the state, and only fishermen employed by the state are allowed to catch them. The caviar is taken to state canning factories, and most of it is then sold abroad.

There has always been a black market for caviar in Russia. This used to be supplied by fishermen who wanted to supplement their incomes. Today the mafia controls illegal fishing and has turned it into a multimillion-dollar business, making use of international connections to distribute the caviar abroad. The mafia have built their own canning factories and stolen or copied state labels and cans to make their caviar look official. In the past people fishing illegally for sturgeon risked getting caught by the police. At worst they were jailed; usually they were only given a fine. Today they may be caught by crime lords, who are more of a threat than the police. They do not like losing business, and they issue severe punishments.

conform to the Communist party's views. For example, foreign films and books were banned because the Party wanted to give the impression that life was no better in noncommunist countries than in Communist ones.

Mikhail Gorbachev's policy of *glasnost* finally gave the media some freedom to reveal the truth about events at home and abroad. Since 1991 the media have been allowed to print and broadcast whatever they want. Foreign films can now be shown in theaters, and foreign books and magazines are on sale in stores. Teachers, too, are free to teach anything in their classes.

Money is in short supply, but there is greater choice in stores. Foreign goods, once banned, can now be sold openly instead of on the black market. Many stores are now privately run. Up-scale department stores and Western-style supermarkets have opened in Moscow and St. Petersburg, and they will soon spread to all the other major cities.

Religious life is also benefiting from the end of communism. After the 1917 revolution, the Communist party declared the USSR an atheist country. It discouraged people from following their religions, abolished religious holidays and festivals, and closed most places of worship. Today people are free to follow their faiths again, though now religion has little meaning for most of them.

A young entrepreneur sells foreign goods that were banned under communism. Now they are a common sight.

The Patriarch, the head of the Russian Orthodox Church, attends an outdoor church service. This service would not have been permitted under communism.

Although Russia has built many huge apartment buildings like the ones on the right, housing is still in short supply. The young woman in the photograph above shares a cramped apartment with her children and her mother.

HOUSING SHORTAGE

Russia suffers from a very serious housing shortage. In 1917 less than 20 percent of the population lived in cities. When the USSR broke up in 1991, this figure had risen to 60 percent. By the year 2000 it is expected to be closer to 75 percent.

To cope with the increasing demand for city homes, the Communist party built large housing projects. Many of these are now in poor condition. They were built badly in the first place, and they have suffered years of neglect because the Communist party concentrated more on building new apartments than on repairing existing ones.

Although thousands of projects have been constructed, there are still not enough of them. Grandparents have to live with their children, and newlyweds remain with their parents. All the apartments inside the projects are small because as many homes as possible had to be provided.

The housing shortage has been made worse by the return of Russian soldiers and their families from the former Eastern Bloc countries, where they are no longer welcome. Refugees from wars in CIS countries along Russia's borders have also added to the problem.

41

POPULATION AND HEALTH		
	births per 1,000 people	deaths per 1,000 people
1900	57	32
1950	25	15
1992	15	11

HEALTH AND WELFARE

There is a basic social security and health system for everyone in Russia. Before 1993 the state paid for this. Now it is financed by contributions from employers. Many of them, including very large firms, are in debt and they cannot meet these payments. As a result, the government, which is itself bankrupt, has less money than it needs to

LIFE EXPECTANCY	
Males:	....64.7 years
Females:	....73.7 years

(Source: 1989 census)

These men have stopped to quench their thirst at a roadside beer stall. As in other countries, the stresses of modern life have driven many Russians to drinking.

provide decent pensions and to invest in hospitals. Many senior citizens have to resort to begging to make ends meet. Russia has 47 doctors and 137 hospital beds per 10,000 people – double the figures for the United States – yet health care is poor because there is a severe shortage of essential equipment and medicine in hospitals.

Many Russians are overweight and have poor diets. Low incomes and high prices mean that people have to economize by buying cheap, fatty meat and starchy food to fill themselves up. The stresses of daily life in the 1990s have driven many people to drinking heavily. President Gorbachev tried to limit the sale of vodka to reduce drunkenness, but this made him so unpopular that he was forced to back down.

Another increasing problem since the end of communism is the spread of illegal drugs. Their use has been encouraged by mafia

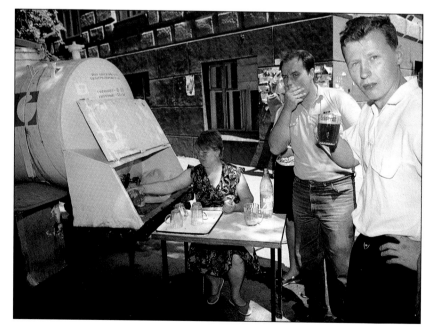

42

black marketeers who are earning fortunes by selling drugs within Russia and the CIS, as well as by exporting them to Europe.

EDUCATION

It is compulsory for children to go to school for ten years, between the ages of seven and seventeen. In the USSR all schools and colleges were owned by the state. After its breakup, some private schools opened. In 1992, 20,000 pupils were being educated privately in 300 schools and 40 colleges. However, the vast majority of children still attend government schools and colleges, which are usually free, although some colleges began charging low fees in 1992.

Once again, because the government is short of money, all its schools and colleges lack good facilities and equipment. The teachers themselves frequently do not get paid because the government has run out of money. Some colleges can keep going only by making their staff open businesses, such as selling cars or furniture.

LITERACY	
Age 15+:	98%
(Source: 1989 census)	

These schoolchildren are learning about the United Kingdom. In the past, the Communist party did not allow teachers to tell their pupils what noncommunist countries were really like because it wanted children to believe that communism was the best form of government.

43

Russia's Cyrillic Alphabet			
RUSSIAN	ENGLISH	RUSSIAN	ENGLISH
а	a father	р	r run
б	b but	с	s sing
в	v van	т	t ten
г	g got	у	u food
д	d dog	ф	f fan
е	ye yet	х	kh loch
ё	yo your	ц	ts bits
ж	zh treasure	ч	ch chin
з	z zoo	ш	sh shop
и	i meet	щ	shch fresh
й	y yellow	ъ	(silent)
к	k kind	ы	y ill
л	l long	ь	(silent)
м	m mad	э	e end
н	n not	ю	yu use
о	o more	я	ya yard
п	p pig		

Above *Russia's Cyrillic alphabet with English equivalents and guides to pronunciation.*

GOVERNMENT AND POLITICS

In the USSR, people could only vote for members of the Communist party; no other political parties were allowed. Voting in elections was compulsory: failure to vote resulted in punishment. Russia's leader, President Yeltsin, aimed to make the country democratic and capitalist. However, his reforms were blocked by Parliament, many of whose members were ex-Communists reluctant to accept change. In September 1993 Yeltsin lost patience with Parliament and closed it. He ordered elections in which the people would be given the opportunity to agree with or to reject his proposed changes. In December 1993 the majority of voters supported Yeltsin's new constitution.

Russia will continue to have a president as its leader. He or she will be elected every four years; the next presidential elections are scheduled for 1996. The president appoints a prime minister, who chooses a government with the president's agreement. The government is responsible for the everyday running of Russia. Its performance is monitored by a new parliament, composed of two houses: an upper house, called the Federation Council, and a lower house, the Duma.

The elections in December 1993 were the first democratic ones since the end of communism. Distrustful of their politicians, only about 55 percent of the people voted, since voting is no longer compulsory. Thirteen major political parties competed for seats in

One of the major improvements in modern Russia is greater freedom of expression. The Communist party did not approve of rock music and would have made it very difficult for this group to perform.

Far left Soldiers cast their votes during the elections on December 12, 1993.

the new parliament. Russia's Choice, which supports President Yeltsin, won fewer seats than the Liberal Democratic Party of Russia, which opposes his plans. Many people are concerned that, like its predecessor, the new parliament will hinder Yeltsin's proposals for a speedy introduction of a market economy. The new constitution gives the president the power to close Parliament and to rule Russia with a government of his own choice. People are now worried that if President Yeltsin were to use this power, Russia's democracy would be short-lived and there would be a return to one-party rule, just like there was in the old days of the USSR.

Leaders exchange abuse in public but make deals behind closed doors; they preach belt-tightening reforms but look well-dressed; and each proclaims himself a "patriot" but seems incapable of improving the quality of life.

Russia's 150 million people are so burdened with hyperinflation, food shortages, lack of fuel for winter and other hardships that few will have the time or interest to follow the deliberations at the Congress [old Parliament]. – **Tony Barber,** **Independent (London),** *November 29, 1992*

Glossary

Censorship   Keeping information secret.

Cold war   The rivalry that existed between the USSR and the United States from the end of the 1940s until the late 1980s.

Consumer goods   Things made by industries to satisfy people's wants.

Corruption   Dishonesty.

Coup   A rebellion to overthrow a government.

Eastern Bloc   The Communist East European countries controlled by the USSR after World War II.

Glasnost   The Russian word for openness. It is used to describe the reforms Gorbachev introduced to make the USSR more honest about life within the USSR and abroad.

Heavy industries   Industries concerned with the production of metals and machinery and the extraction of natural resources.

Iron Curtain   The term used by Winston Churchill to describe the division of Europe into Communist and noncommunist countries after World War II.

Perestroika   The Russian word used to describe the restructuring of the USSR's industries under Gorbachev's leadership.

Permafrost   Ground that is frozen all year, the top layer of which melts in the summer sun and then refreezes in autumn.

Republic   A country or a region within a country that has its own president and government.

Revolution   A rebellion that overthrows a government or a ruler and completely changes political organization.

Rubbish tip   Landfill.

Steppe   A band of flat grasslands with fertile black soil.

Subsidies   Money paid to industries by a government to keep prices low.

Taiga   The Russian word for the coniferous forests that form a wide belt across the center of the country.

Tundra   A treeless wasteland with bitterly cold winters. The subsoil of the tundra is frozen all year round.

Further information

Further information on environmental problems can be obtained from Greenpeace and Friends of the Earth. Survival International is taking an active interest in the future of the native people of Siberia. Other topical issues are reported in newspapers and magazines, such as *National Geographic*.

BOOKS

Clark, Mary J. *The Commonwealth of Independent States*. Headliners. Brookfield, CT: Millbrook Press, 1992.

Department of Geography Staff. *The Soviet Union in Pictures*. Visual Geography Series. Minneapolis: Lerner Publications, 1989.

Hawkes, Nigel. *Glasnost and Peristroika*. World Issues. Vero Beach, FL: Rourke Corp., 1990.

Magosci, Paul R. *Russian Americans*. The Peoples of North America. New York: Chelsea House, 1989.

Ross, Stewart. *The Russian Revolution 1914–1924*. Witness History. New York: Bookwright Press, 1989.

Schecter, Kate S. *Boris Yeltsin*. Junior World Biographies. New York: Chelsea House, 1993.

Solzhenitsyn, Aleksandr. *One Day in the Life of Ivan Denisovich*. New York: Bantam Books, 1984.

Stewart, Gail B. *The Soviet States*. Places in the News. New York: Crestwood House, 1992.

Sullivan, George. *Mikhail Gorbachev*. Rev. Ed. New York: Simon & Schuster Trade, 1990.

FILMS

Anna Karenina (1935) The wife of a Russian aristocrat falls in love with a cavalry officer.

Gorky Park (1983) Moscow police link murders with a sable-smuggling operation.

Reds (1981) An American journalist gets involved in the Russian Revolution.

The Russia House (1990) A British publisher finds himself caught between allied intelligence and the Russians when he is given a manuscript.

PICTURE ACKNOWLEDGMENTS
Maps were provided by Peter Bull. The artwork on page 44 was provided by John Yates.
Photographs: Archiv für Kunst und Gesichte 10; Bryan and Cherry Alexander 5, 29; Associated Press/Topham 31; Camera Press Limited 8 (top), 15, 30, 36, 44; David Cumming 4, 11, 18, 19, 21, 22, 26-27, 28, 32, 37, 38, 39, 40, 41 (right), 42, 43; Eye Ubiquitous 20 (Gary Trotter); Robert Harding 1; Impact Photos 17 (Paul Forster), 25 (Andrei Solomonov), 41 (left, Peter Arkell); Rex Features Limited 3, 14, 35; Frank Spooner Pictures 9, 13; John Massey Stewart 7, 8 (bottom), 33 (V. E. Flint), 45.

Index

The figures in **bold** refer to photographs and maps.